ALL THE FLOWERS KNEELING

ALL THE FLOWERS KNEELING

PAUL TRAN

PENGUIN POETS

PENGUIN BOOKS

An imprint of Penguin Random House LLC

penguinrandomhouse.com

LIBRARY OF CONGRESS CATALOGING-IN-PUBLICATION DATA

Names: Tran, Paul, (Poet) author.

Title: All the flowers kneeling / Paul Tran.

Description: New York : Penguin, [2022] | Series: Penguin poets |

Identifiers: LCCN 2021027962 (print) | LCCN 2021027963 (ebook) |

ISBN 9780143136842 (paperback) | ISBN 9780525508342 (ebook)

Subjects: LCGFT: Poetry.

Classification: LCC PS3620.R3627 A78 2022 (print) | LCC PS3620.R3627

(ebook) | DDC 811/.6—dc23

LC record available at https://lccn.loc.gov/2021027962

LC ebook record available at https://lccn.loc.gov/2021027963

Printed in the United States of America

1st Printing

Set in Electra, with display in Knockout

CONTENTS

v

ALL THE FLOWERS KNEELING

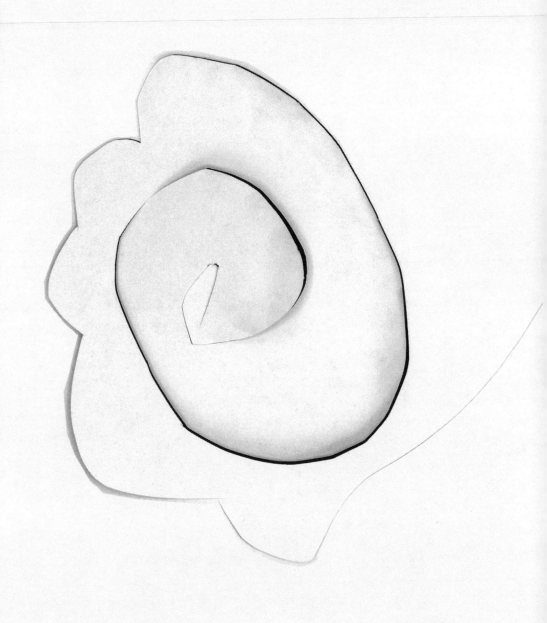

Modes of knowledge
light/dark
religion
transcendentalism
science
memory
art history
music
storytelling

family/generational

self awareness
pop culture

ORCHARD OF KNOWING

[handwritten: kind of tetrameter?]

Into the shadows I go
and find you, gorgeous as your necklace *[handwritten: Evisceration as Jewelerization]*
  of nine hundred and ninety-nine index fingers.
All of them point at me
  as the kill to complete your mission:
to return to your kingdom by returning to your king
  a thousand human sacrifices.
You chase me. You swing your sword *[handwritten: Drama!]*

  yet I remain beyond your reach.
I'll surrender, I tell you,
  when you detach from your received idea of purpose.
So you do. You set down your weapon.
  But I didn't mean the blade in your hand.
I meant the blade in your mind.

[handwritten left margin annotations: I / You / Me / Your / I/me / I/your / I/You / you/Your / I/You]

1

INCIDENT REPORT

I had a form.

The form said *Name of victim*.

The form named me.

The form was a form of naming.

Naming gave me form.

The form said *Time of incident*.

Time could be measured.

The Incident could be defined.

Both had a form.

Both were a form of naming.

The form said *Age*.

Age could be measured by Time.

Age could be defined by the Incident.

The Incident occurred on the night before my twenty-first birthday.

The Time was night as night became night.

The Incident occurred in my room at the Time.

The Time occurred to me after the Incident.

The form said *Race or ethnicity*.

Both were constructs.

Both marked me.

Both had a form.

Both were a form of naming.

Naming was marking.

Process of reconstructing self after trauma

I marked the form.

(Asian. Bottom. 4 Now.)

I was a construct.

(Looking 4 Fun. No Strings Attached.)

I was unremarkable.

The form said *Sex*.

The form listed my options.

I had no option.

I went along with the Sex.

The Sex had a Name.

(I won't say the Name.)

Both marked me.

The form said *Affiliation*.

Everything started out fine.

The form said *Residence*.

I unlocked the door.

I misread *Affiliation* as *Affliction*.

The Name entered.

I misread *Residence* as *Residual*.

The Name kissed me.

The form said *Alcohol or drugs used at the time of incident*.

I was having a good time.

The form said *Relationship with the assailant prior to incident*.

I did the thing I was good at.

The form said *Type of coercion or force involved*.

The Name hit me.

The form said *Please specify*.

The Name choked me.

The form said *Ability to consent was inhibited by*.

The Name pressed a white towel against my face. *doesn't answer question*

The form said *Please specify*.

The towel smelled like sugar.

Please specify.

An ice cream truck drove by.

(Please.)

I heard the song. *deviation*

4

SCHEHERAZADE/SCHEHERAZADE

1

Waking again to the spartan
furnishing—brass
knobs and coat hooks, curtain

moth-gnawed and yellowing, plastic mattress
atop a twin frame, photograph of me and my mother
turned away, book from a class

on empire and literature
that told the story of a story-
teller who evades the end awaiting her

each morning by giving the king not her body
but her imagination each night
for a thousand and one nights—what humiliated me

as I relived my death in that room without sunrise
wasn't my desire for light but my desire for more darkness.

5

2

Except for the glow of distant ships

nothing could be seen.

My mother, staring into

the dark, waiting for the light

as she waited years ago

for another ship to take her from her

life, adjusted her glasses.

The past came into view:

line of women. Line of soldiers.

Red sand beach. Sand red with

blood. Waves racing in.

A soldier. His rifle. My mother

on her knees. Waves retreating.

Once upon a time, she began.

Making peace at night

3

In a version of the story there's no ocean. No waves racing in. No waves retreating.
Their behavior neither the behavior of memory nor the past. In a version of the story

there's no soldier. No rifle. No bullet wound marking skull after skull like a period
at the end of a sentence. No final thought for each prisoner. In a version of the story

there's no sand. No beach. No adjective to modify or justify the washed-away
blood. No propaganda for beauty. No grotesque agenda. In a version of the story

there's no line of women robbed of their womanhood. No prayers. No answering
bodhisattva. No means to know if no answer is the answer. In a version of the story

there's no ship. No going forward. No getting back. No inner compass or magnetic field
or spinning needle or stars to tell my mother where she is. In a version of the story

there's no story. No sleepless dawn. No twilight. *Nothing happened.* My mother disappears
whatever blights her the way she now makes her living: altering and tailoring the story

as though the truth were trousers to be hemmed. She changes and is changed by how
she tells her story. There is no truth. Only a version. A version. A verge. A vengeance.

Spins story until it gains meaning

4

With him I had an audience. Both heads
at attention. Ravenous. A kind of ravishing. *Tell me*
you like it. I told him I liked it. *Tell me how bad*

you want it. I told him I wanted it bad, maybe,
because I did want, badly, to
be remade, changed so thoroughly

at the core of my being, the corridor through
which he entered like a king,
though he was far from a king, and in doing so

took me, at least part of me, with him. I was willing
by then, by force, to entertain my executioner.
I stopped punching. Kicking. Resisting

what I couldn't resist. What he wanted to hear
I told him. I made my pussy talk. I found in violence a voice.

5

Across the table from my mother
I filled two cups with tea.
We sat in silence. We sipped in silence.
Her silence demanding mine.
Some suffering we'd rather not know
so we don't suffer knowledge
calling on us in the name of love,
to blame ourselves and to appropriate the pain

because we think of pain and blame
as objects requiring purpose and possession.
That's not love. That has no name.
We finished our tea. We set down our cups.
What do you see? Leaves. Water.
Waves. Ships. Bodies. Bullets. No shore.

6

Let me be clear. *Obama?*

Inside this story is another story.

The frame is a door.

Behind the door is another door.

Both the room and the king are literal and figurative.

To use figurative language is to make an argument. *real*

Like Scheherazade my mother and I cleave to and from our story.

Like Scheherazade ours is a story of refrain.

The word *refrain* means not just *resist* but also *repetition*.

Repetition is emphasis. *music?*

The emphasis being the purpose for repetition.

My purpose is precision.

Even when I'm unclear I'm deliberate. *real*

When I'm deliberate I'm liberated. *so real*

Night after night A
I returned to the room. Windows closed. Drapes drawn. B
Neither spring nor starlight A

to ignite the air. Only his breath lingering on B
the pillowcase. His face C
in the mirror like the image of a swan B

in a lake. I was the lake C
doubling and doubting his image. Could I understand D
what happened if I understood him? Could I slake my rage C

if I knew what the next day had planned? D
To-go containers. Emails. Pills. Laundry. More laundry. E
At the foot of the bed, I decided D

there had to be a way
out. There *was* the way out. E
Y

Escape!

SCIENTIFIC METHOD

book of human anatomy from 1500s

Of the books he wrote about me, my favorite is the book Master had
bound with my skin. *De humani corporis fabrica.* Am I vain?
    Born poor. Illiterate. Oblivious to any life but this,
never did I expect perpetuity. Never did I expect a man to want me

implication
    the way he wanted me. Master didn't care
how ugly I was. My nose flat. My thighs fat. My teeth
    the color of horse shit. Master dug me out
from the ground. He took my corpse into his arms. He held me so close

    I forgot I was a body. I became his body
of work. Biology. Physiology. Anatomy. Master, doubting
    the Old Masters, believed doubt could draw a new map to the interior.
In his classroom at the university, Master had me undressed and laid

    on a table for his pupils
to see. He descended from his dais with the dynamism of a god
    walking among his disciples. Whatever he dictated they scribbled
on their slates, lapping his theories and thoughts

    like dogs lapping piss from a chamber pot.
Some want to be holy. Some want to be human. Some want to believe
    the nature of the human revealed reveals the nature of the holy.
As Master opened me—groin hard

    against my hips, hands in my guts—I opened him. I gave him
nerve. Tendon. Muscle. Ventricle. Mandible. Sternum. Tibia. Atria. Labia.
    Every aspect of myself
I hadn't resource or reason to fathom—heft of the mind, mechanics

    of the heart—he dissected. Documented. Paraded
before his surgical circus. His spectators and skeptics
    oohing and aahing. Shuffling in their seats. Fanning back the heat.
Their interest with what was found in me formed

from their interest with what could be in them . . .
I wanted to tell them that
    they weren't special. They had no soul
beyond their investment in the function of the soul. Their gaze

not absolute. Not pure. Not empirical. Only imperial. Impure. Approximate.
I wanted to tell them that there was much
    they'd never know. They thought they knew
what knowledge was. But knowledge

    was me: the edge of doubt and belief, of what persists
Master after Master, reified and repudiated, preserved
    in a Providence library—air-conditioned, light-controlled—
touched and retouched, awaiting a new Master to approach the edge.

THE NIGHTMARE: OIL ON CANVAS: HENRY FUSELI: 1781

sick ass painting

Too hot to

    rest, I toss

        my arms off   *woah!*

the bed. My night- *oh*

    gown wet with

        sweat. I feel you

—a sack of

    scavenged skulls

        on my chest

—sipping

    the salt from

        my breasts. Imp.

Incubus. Im-

    pulse. You and

        me like a mare

that must be

    broken in

        by breaking in-

to. Tamed is

    how fire is

        by giving itself

something to destroy:

    it destroys it-

        self. Who

can deter-

    mine what's inside

        another?

What is risked

    when we enter?

        Caliper. Forceps.

Scalpel. Oculus.

    Perhaps you're

        the wilderness

that waits with-

    in me. Perhaps an-

other mystery, I
open beneath
        you. Yoked. Harnessed.
                Paralyzed.
At once a-
        wake and a-
                sleep. I nay.
I knock
        over the kerosene
                lamp. Light of
the rational
        mind snuffed. Shadow
                of shadows.
Because I can't
        see, I sense.
                Your thumb
thrumming
        my mouth. A
                command. Arch-
angel. Vision
        of invasion.
                Insemination.

BIOLUMINESCENCE

There's a dark so deep beneath the sea the creatures beget their own
light. This feat, this fact of adaptation, I could say, is beautiful

though the creatures are hideous. Lanternfish. Hatchetfish. Viperfish.
I, not unlike them, forfeited beauty to glimpse the world hidden

by eternal darkness. I subsisted on falling matter, unaware
from where or why matter fell, and on weaker creatures beguiled

by my luminosity. My hideous face opening, suddenly, to take them
into a darkness darker and more eternal than this underworld

underwater. I swam and swam toward nowhere and nothing.
I, after so much isolation, so much indifference, kept going

even if going meant only waiting, hovering in place. So far below, so far
away from the rest of life, the terrestrial made possible by and thereby

dependent upon light, I did what I had to do. I stalked. I killed.
I wanted to feel in my body my body at work, working to stay

alive. I swam. I kept going. I waited. I found myself without meaning
to, without contriving meaning at the time, in time, in the company

of creatures who, hideous like me, had to be their own illumination.
Their own god. Their own genesis. Often we feuded. Often we fused

like anglerfish. Blood to blood. Desire to desire. We were wild. Bewildered.
Beautiful in our wilderness and wildness. In the most extreme conditions

we proved that life can exist. *I exist. I am my life*, I thought, approaching
at last the bottom of the sea. It wasn't the bottom. It wasn't the sea.

[handwritten annotation:] When its like a metaphor or something

[handwritten annotation:] What was it?

[handwritten annotation:] This one is for real animal fans who prefer more dark and twisted types of animals

HYPOTHESIS

Whether it's true
that the moth mistakes the candle's flame
for the moon or the bioluminescent
pheromones of another moth,

I can't say.
I was the candle.
I was the flame

conceived in and by reason of
darkness, nibbling on a darkening wick.
When moth after moth after moth
swarmed me with their powdery wings,

I asked why.
I asked how.
I asked if

I could survive knowing
that not everything has a reason,
that not everything is capable
of or interested in reason.

Nothing answered.
Nothing spoke
my language of smoke.

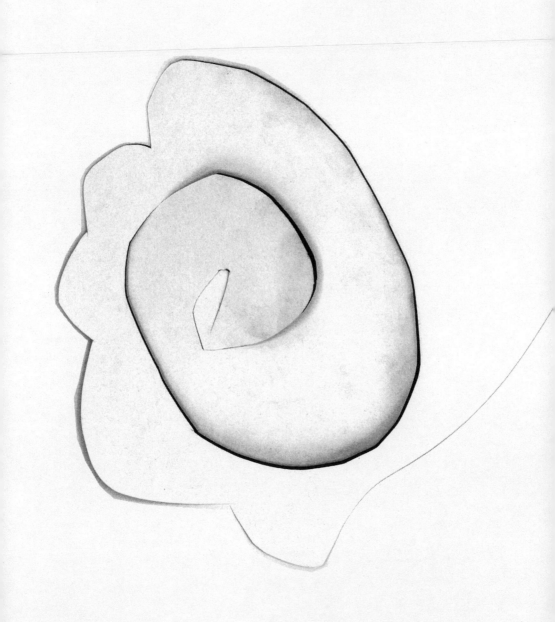

THE CAVE

Someone standing at the mouth had the idea
to enter. To go farther

than light or language could.
As they followed
the idea, light and language followed

like two wolves—panting, hearing
the panting. A shapeless scent
in the damp air . . .

Keep going, the idea said.

Someone kept going. Deeper and deeper, they saw
others had been there. Others had left

objects that couldn't have found their way
there alone. Ochre-stained shells. Bird bones. Ground hematite.
On the walls,

as if stepping into history, someone saw
their purpose. Cows. Bulls. Bison. Deer. Horses—
some pregnant, some slaughtered.

The wild-
life seemed wild and alive, moving

when someone moved, casting their shadows
on the shadows stretching
in every direction. *Keep going,*

the idea said again. Go . . .

Someone continued. They followed the idea so far inside that
outside became another idea.

21

PROVENANCE

There she was
       in that lavender dress,
           in that room,
in that apartment,
       turning around
           to answer
his fist
       pounding that door
           in the middle of that day
that must've been a day
       in August,
           the start of that season
when all around them,
       all that could be
           changed by violence
and violently changed,
       the hills and the valley,
           the canyons and the cliffs
tongue-kissed
       by the Santa Ana,
           burst into bright
seams of silver smoke,
       and though it was
           unclear how he burst
through that door,
       why her dress fell
           to that floor
like that flame and flash
       lashing the bed-
           straw and the sunflowers
until the flowers bent
       their heads from the sun,
           or what they saw
in each other
       —who was whose

[handwritten annotation: violence inside and outside frame]

[handwritten annotation: war?]

horse, rider, ride, reins, neck
pulled, pulling, arching, arched
back like the curves
of that wildfire's hips,
that scorched hour
grinding into
the next, there,
in that room,
in that apartment—
my mother and father
became my mother and father
and, the next spring,
for the first time,
brought me home
through that entryway
that was neither
a way in nor a way out
of that violence,
that pounding,
that answer,
that turning around
to discover,
so clearly,
all that
would not change.

CHROME

[handwritten: traumatized father?]

Years he lives alone on Montezuma Road. Delivers newspapers

during dawn's darkest hours. Marine layer hangs like gunfire

over the Gulf of Tonkin. Optical illusion: how cleverly the War begins *[handwritten: double meaning]*

in his '93 Mazda MPV. We sail I-15 South as though it's the Thu Bồn River,

flee Hội An's cinnamon forest barricade, viscera-flooded streets.

American soldiers peeling his house apart, straw by straw.

His uncles wearing nothing but name tags around their necks, lying

in a ditch of saw-toothed rocks. Flies spewing from a missing eye.

We grab donuts at a panadería in North Park. A boom box beneath

La Virgen coos "Como La Flor" while I probe a glazed exit wound:

wedding ring he never gave my mother. Too poor for love. Too ruined

for ritual. I dance with him. My feet atop his feet. Shadow in his shadow.

Our song doesn't end even when it does. Even when Yolanda pushes a bullet *[handwritten: lives new work]*

through Selena's back. We keep going. We remount his chrome motorboat

as daylight singes sheets of warm air, revealing another imitation of Heaven.

My father in the rearview mirror: sky I go blind scouring for the sun. *[handwritten: linked to abuse imagery]*

[handwritten: Trauma affects ability to form parent/child dynamic]

24

OUR LADY OF THE SACRED HEART

Unlike you, I couldn't claim Gabriel came
in a dream. I had no conceivable evidence. *Jesus or father?*

My father finished. He turned on the TV. *deflection*
With him, even the winter air invades me. *abuse/violence*

LANDSCAPE WITH THE FALL OF ICARUS: OIL ON CANVAS: PIETER BRUEGEL THE ELDER: 1560

Given that the door had to be opened and closed,
the jeans unbuttoned and unzipped, the right hand placed over my mouth
while the left hand held me, held me

there, held me down, I can't help
but think, again then, then and again, that
suffering, its human position, isn't entirely random

because someone has to decide, at some point, with purpose
or not, that they're going to get
what they want or what they tell themselves they want

in order to get what they really want
even if it means hurting another, even if it means hurting them both,
even if they can't discern what they really want

or that they're hurting, yet,
until the hurt and the want, lacking
explanation, or eluding it, become indiscernible

from the rest of their suffering, confused for and eclipsing
that suffering, the way the story of sunlight melting wax wings
is confused for the story of hubris and eclipses the story of the child

following the father, as the child was instructed to,
from one dungeon to another
of sky, and given that, given all that followed

when I followed my father
from our dungeon to one of men
not unlike my father and me, I could've blamed him

for the him who followed, could've maintained the story
that it was neither sunlight nor hubris
that defeated me but descent

while bystanders stood by, and I could've reframed
the defeat as the defect of wings, my descent as my dissent to flight,
and though I did, though I did whenever and however

to suit my schemes, my shifting schema,
I accept, for now, just now, that
in the story it was me, and only me, falling from the sky

to the sea, that as I struggled against my end
I struggled, too, against the fact, falling
and falling, that the end would end, and as I fell

from one blue dungeon to another, I saw
as I fell closer and closer
to the end, the instant preceding the end

when everything could still be changed, in the infinite blue of the water
the infinite blue of the sky
and my face, my father's face and his, looking back.

*above
↓
escape*

Title really helps to tell the story, just like in painting

THE FIRST LAW OF MOTION

An object in motion stays in motion

From the photograph of us in the kitchen
I cut my father's face. The denim shirt

hugging his sun-scorched skin. His hands on my shoulders
as I blow out the two .99 candles.
Was it a surprise

I turned out like him?
Exacting. Stubborn. Attention-seeking. Resentful of longing

I could not sate. My mind

a dull knife sharpened by a dull knife
until both dulled further, dividing
into perfect triangles the cake. My heart

a cabinet door swung open
to reveal plates neatly stacked
and then slammed shut.

I sought to determine how and what
he left. The impact on me

it had. Would have. Continues even now to have

despite the control I've sought to establish
over everyone and everything, including my longing
for control . . . Yet I couldn't

cut him from me. Cut me from him.

By what force will my longing be stopped?

Time. Distance. Clarity.
Even after he turned from me, after he reached for
and stuffed into my mouth

the white towel, the last thing
from that night
I remember, the man

—whose hesitancy resembled my father's

the afternoon my father left
me at the park with a box of leftover KFC—
failed to stop

the pattern of recklessness. Wretchedness. Wreckage. Regret
brought on by my longing, my failure

to locate the regret and the longing
beneath that. I took the knife. The scissors. The shears.
Anything to carve past

the past, the body I hated

because I was not so much exhausted as I was
just bored of feeling everything and nothing
at all. At once. At last,

gash after gash, I reached inside.
Wrists. Hips. Thighs. I found
not the source of my regret. Not the force to stop it.

Just more.

Until acted upon by an unbalanced force

All night I wait for the cactus flower to bloom.

I wait, as if the cactus flower and the night both know

I'm waiting, asking also to bloom not in spite of light

but simply in darkness, to bloom that simply, briefly, almost

randomly, and then immediately to wither without return.

I'm asking to live like that. I'm asking—after a life of asking

for permanence, for another chance to prove

the consequence of longing isn't always regret,

that longing to control my life means not controlling longing

but letting go of regret, longing, and consequence

so I could be free, set myself free even of letting go and waiting

for permission—to live. Immediate. Random. Brief.

Nothing blooms. Nothing withers. Only the knowledge

that there's a difference between letting go and setting free.

Retelling of life in 3 parts- abuse, rape, freedom

SCIENTIFIC METHOD

Of course I chose the terry cloth surrogate.
Milkless artifice. False idol.
Everyone, I'm told, has a mother,

but Master bred me
in a laboratory, his colony of orphans.
Rhesus macaque. *Macaca mulatta.* Old World   *white supremacy / western dominati*

monkeys, my matriarchs ruled
the grasslands and forests long before men like him
weaned their whiteness

from our chromosomes, slashed and burned
our home, what they once called
the Orient. French Indochina. Việt Nam. Master,
pre colonial → colonial → post-colonial
like a good despot, besotted
and dumbstruck, dying
to discern the genesis of allegiance, the science of love

and loss, nature versus nurture, segregated me at birth
from my maker, pelt sopping
with placental blood. In a chamber

where he kept track of me, his pupils   *→ seen this before*
recorded my every movement, every utterance, hoping
I might evince to them a part of themselves.

But I wasn't stupid.   *→ rebellious instead of blindly loyal this time*
I knew famine and emaciation,
and nevertheless I picked that lifeless piece of shit

because it was soft to hold. Though it couldn't hold me,
I clung to the yellow-faced devil
as though it was my true mother

and I grasped the true function of motherhood: *evokes monkey*
witness to my suffering, companion in hell.   *in cage*
Unlike infants with wire mothers   *experiments*

I didn't hurl myself on the floor
in terror or tantrum, rocking back and forth,
colder than a corpse. I had

what Master believed to be
a psychological base of operations. Emotional
attachment. Autonomy. Everything

what happens to a human treated inhumanely?

he denied and did to me, his ceaseless cruelty
concealed as inquisition, unthinkable
until it was thought, I endured

by keeping for myself the wisdom
he yearned to discover and take credit for.
Love, like me, is a beast

→ finds power in language thats not usually positive

no master can maim. No dungeon can discipline.
Love is at once master and dungeon.
So don't underestimate me.

Simpleminded and subservient as I might appear
to be, I gathered more about Master
than he did about me, which, I guess, is a kind of fidelity

conceived not from fondness but from fear
magnified by fascination. Master made me his
terry cloth surrogate, his red-clawed

god, nursing his id on my tits,
and for that, I pitied him. All this time
he was the animal. All this time he belonged to me.

reclamation of self after abuse

Fall

To the underworld,
I went with the god. I was gullible.
Promising. He promised me
a replica of the world

where nothing died
because everything—the orchard,
the apples, the pomegranates—
was already dead.

At the center of my new life
there was a bed. A bell
I rang when I was hungry
for his attention. I felt alive

for the first time, in love
though what we made, what he made
my body do with his body,
day and night, night and day, wasn't *love*.

If being his meant being mine
then I chose what wasn't a choice:
I swallowed his seed.
I stayed to stay alive. Never mind

the details I missed—
smell of witchgrass, chatter of people
living for the first and only time—
except that I missed being missed.

Winter

White thread pulled through the needle's eye.

    Another wedding dress restitched. Telling me
        that to survive the past is to leave it behind,

my mother reminded me of Ngài Mục Kiền Liên:

    how he snuck into Hell to feed his mother a bowl of rice.
        Like white thread pulled through a needle's eye
the grains caught fire as he lifted the spoon each time

    to her mouth. The monk traded his soul so that his mother
        might survive and leave her past sins behind
for a future that would hurt in ways neither could foresee.

    Am I him? Am I the mother? Am I waiting for *my* mother
        —a white thread pulled through a needle's eye—

to save *me*, to trade her future for mine? My mother, bridled

    to motherhood, though never a bride in a dress white as rice,
        left me her past to survive. She left me behind

in Hell, where I had to find a way to save us both.

    Mother. Child. Monk. Mortal. Needle. Eye.
        The white thread pulled through the needle's eye.

It's not the past we must survive. It is the past we leave behind.

Spring

A morning in April 1975.

A girl in her yellow áo dài.

Her mother not saying, *Goodbye.*

Stay. Come back.

Her back turned to the only world she knows.

The lover she'll never see again.

The shore with no keel in sight.

Thương anh thì thương rất nhiều

mà ván đã đóng thuyền rồi.

There's no way to enter the underworld and leave unchanged.

Death changed me.

Death takes not the body but the mind.

In my mind, I come back to my mother. I stay.

Say goodbye.

Summer

At the edge of the orchard, amid shadow and light
      snaking not like snakes as they move

but like snakes as they slough their skins
      so that the self left behind and the self moving on

appear, at enough distance, sometimes
      up close, without inspection, identical, I saw

a baby bird, dead, or dying, that the ants had begun
      to dismantle, mouthful by mouthful, like a lie

from a belief, and I thought, though not
      entirely true except insofar as truth is, or is

required, that the mother should've saved her
      child, shouldn't have expected the child to save itself

so that, inevitably, the mother could be saved
      from the inevitable, that which will, by its will, against

our will, occur and recur, but I knew, having been
      a baby bird left for dead, for death, that nobody

is saved or safe, that survival, defined as the fact
      of continuing to live or exist, typically in spite

of an incident, is, by that definition, simply
      the opposite of death, and that what's *not* so

simple is knowing what death is, how sudden
      and often it occurs and recurs, how it can seem

at any point, any distance, like living or existing . . .
      I *want to see the world as it is*. As it is, there, then, alone

at the edge of the orchard, amid light and shadow,
      I had no idea if I'd know, for certain, it was the world.

ENDOSYMBIOSIS

It wasn't him
but what he did
that lived on

inside me.
I had to
learn that.

I had to
cleave *action*
from *figure*,

the verb *do*
from the noun *doll*.
I had to

imagine
the double *ll*
not as two walls

closing in,
two bodies
side by side

in a twin bed,
two mirrors
facing

each other,
two tally marks
for the first and second

time I was . . .
but a road
through

Hell—this
near contraction
of *he* and *will*—

[handwritten annotations: closing in / contraction ; do / doll ; hell / he'll / he will ; ellipsis dot dot dot]

where the punctuation
could so easily
be missed.

LIPSTICK ELEGY

of the ocean?

I climb down to the beach facing the Pacific. Torrents of rain
shirr the sand. On the other side, my grandmother sleeps
soundlessly in her bed. Her áo dài of the whitest silk.
My mother knew her mother died before the telephone rang
like bells announcing the last American helicopter leaving Sài Gòn.
Arrow shot back to its bow. Long-distance missile.
She'd leap into the sky to fly home if she could. Instead she works
overtime. Curls her hair with hot rollers. Rouges her cheeks
like Gong Li in *Raise the Red Lantern*. I'm her understudy. Hiding
in the doorway between her grief and mine, I apply her foundation
to my face. I conceal the parts of me she conceals, puckering my lips
as if to kiss a man that loves me the way I want to be loved.
I speak their bewitching names aloud. *Twisted Rose. Fuchsia in Paris. Irreverence.*
I choose the lipstick she'd least approve of. My mouth a pomegranate
split open. A grenade with a loose pin. In the kitchen,
I wrap a white sheet around my waist and dance
for hours, mesmerized by my reflection in a charred skillet.
I laugh her laugh, the way my grandmother laughed
when she taught me to pray the Chú Đại Bi, when I braided her hair
in unbearable heat, my tiny fingers weaving the silver strands
into a fishtail, a French twist. Each knot a future she never named, buried
in the soil of her, where she locked away the image of her sons and daughters
locked away. I'm sorry, mother of my mother, immortal bodhisattva
with a thousand hands, chewing a fist of betel root, your teeth black as dawn.
No child in our family stays a child their mother can love.

prophecy/truth

39

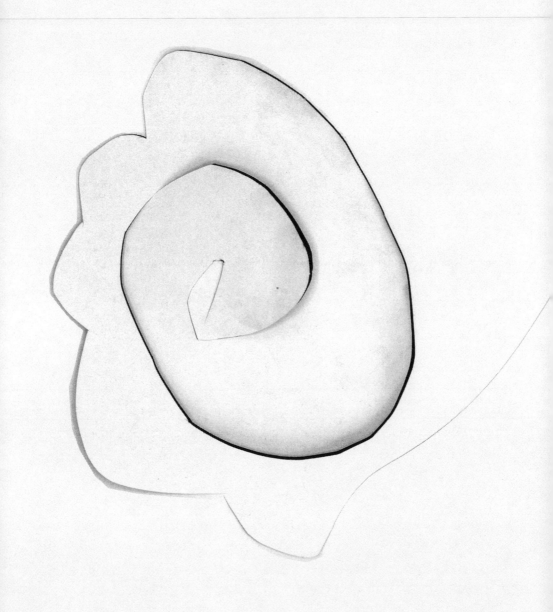

INCANTATION

I write your name
    on a sheet
of paper.
    I fold it
in half.

    In the center
of a bowl:
    Lavender.
Quartz.
    A feather.

With a kitchen knife
    I summon blood
to the surface
    of my left palm.
Love line.

    Life line.
Tell me
    what this means.
I clench my fist.
    I squeeze

a drop of ichor
    over the dead
flowers,
    the rock and plume.
I strike a match.

    To vanquish
you from me
    forever,
I whisper
    into the pyre.

Goodbye.
    I bury

your ash
  in the garden.
Goodbye.

  Winter
to spring.
    Goodbye.
Then summer.
    Nothing blooms

where I keep you.
    Not hoa lan
or birds-of-paradise
    choking
the encroaching fern.

Except me,
    you still kill
everything.

I SEE NOT STARS BUT THEIR LIGHT REACHING ACROSS THE DISTANCE BETWEEN US

disjointed alerts

I walked through the fog-covered field. I was told I could
See the planet visible in the night sky. Jupiter. Saturn. Something   *2*

Not usually visible, like my desire now for the life
Stars have. To be fixed. To be luminous. I knew what I wanted   *2*

But I didn't know how I'd achieve it. The things I loved had lost
Their magnetism, their form and function, like the shadows   *3*
Light once made sharp. Then sharper. Then nothing.

Reaching into my purse, I drew out a cigarette. I sensed
Across the field someone approaching. I couldn't tell who or if   *3*
The field itself was approaching, closing that   *I like this line*

Distance separating belief from doubt. It was at the edge
Between where I stood—waiting, anticipating—with the fog dividing   *∂*

Us, the stranger and me, eliminating all that I didn't need to see.   *1*

Us in the car, in the last hour of light, listening to *Melodrama* as we waited to leave
    The city I escaped to after the incident. The rush hour of being seemed

Stranger and more familiar than I remembered when I first arrived from Providence

    And felt obliterated by the landscape towering over, around, and inside of
        Me. It occurred to me that, suddenly, heading west, chasing the sunset
    Eliminating another day, my sister finding another way through the traffic,

    All thought was a kind of framing, and if I reframed my thinking, I'd find
        That I wasn't leaving a life but driving, fast or slow, toward a new one.

    I hated that: not the thought but how easy it was to believe. I hated that belief
        Didn't erase or redeem the time I spent otherwise convinced. In the tunnel

    Need and what I confused for it grew smaller and smaller, until too small even

To view in the mirror, like the skyline vanishing into the sky. Once, history helped me
See the future. That everything vanished, however, was the price of looking back.

See me at the end of summer, the dean said, and handed me two pamphlets.
The first: Psychological Services. The second: Time Management.
Future and past could be managed by organizing the present into tasks

That, when completed in time, in a satisfactory manner, indicated progress.
Everything was a thing to do well so that others felt comfortable. I was a cell
Vanished from the spreadsheet with each meeting. Pill. Progress report filled.

However, the present persisted. There, like a window, frozen, refusing to close,

Was another progress report. Pill. Meeting. Task to complete. At the clinic
The nurse took my urine sample, my blood sample, and I paid whatever
Price for results entered into a computer. My statement recorded on a pad

Of yellow legal paper that, page after page, went on forever. I calculated,
Looking at my bank account, the cost of progress: No going forward. No turning
Back. I stayed, there, present, managing what I could, trapped in that summer.

Back in the underworld, in bed with another nameless-by-now god, the shadows

I named *What I Got, What I Asked For,* and *What I Really Wanted*

Stayed visible, even in the dark, even after he turned off the light and lay

There, next to me, with me, taking me into his arms. Often another shadow would

Present itself—*What I Accepted*—not absorbing or displacing the others but somehow

Managing to overshadow them. It said, *Call me Master.* It said, *If you do*

What I say, you won't get hurt. That was the problem: again and again

I got hurt. I asked for hurt. Must've wanted to be hurt. I accepted that hurt

Could be a way to heal. A problem was only a problem until I found a way to use it.

Trapped in that logic, in that grip, that faceless-by-now face

In that timeless-because-all-the-time-room looking at, into, and then through me . . .

That was enough to show me, turning on the light hot as the air at the end of another

Summer, the sharp difference between healing and heeling. Parallel lines. A vanishing point.

ugh

this one is bad wno

Summer the year after. Scent of ginkgo. Holly. Us inside the rotunda. The oculus.

The endless champagne. Brown graduation robes. You approached me
Sharp in your suit. A toast. A cheese platter. *Have we met?* You spoke as if we hadn't.

Difference: the little time made. The distance

Between then and now: you next to me. Your hand on mine. I told myself I was
Healing. I ran. The trees hailed their leaves. A car blared its horn.

And wasn't that also forgiveness? Me sparing you. Me not

Heeling you. Me permitting us our secrets. Our separate memories.
Parallel suffering. Stupidity. Shame. The sun set. I filed behind

Lines of proud parents. Babies with balloon animals. Alumni. On stage

A band played a Journey song. On the river flames burst from floating braziers.
Vanishing. Returning. Fire on water. Ships of light. To go on at that

Point—to understand what couldn't be understood—was to set us both free.

Point A: me. Point B: me.

★

To the zoo I schlep through sleet in stilettos. I imagine the snow leopards
Understand theirs to be the only world. They get fed. They get root canals.
What am I to them? To anyone?

★

Couldn't sleep. *Too hot to rest.* The nightmare resumed.

★

Be it known: I entered the economy of abjection. I wanted my pain
Understood. I found an audience. The profit I made
Was all I had to pay the rent. Utilities. Food that passed through me unlike pain.

★

To the penguins amused by my palm on the glass, I'm a blue-green spectrum.

★

Set on stage in my cage of the flesh, my cage of the mind, the performance rendered
Us captive. Captivated. I wanted the audience to see me. I wanted to see myself
Both as I was and as I wasn't. Good survivor. Bad survivor. Since I couldn't be
Free, I chose ambivalence. I renounced expectations. My investment in cause and effect.

survivorship
as performance
for others

Free from freedom, I lived day to day until, just like that, I had a new history.

I scrawled on a napkin a new to-do list. Noon in the garden, I harvested tomatoes.

Chose cilantro for the canh chua my mother, over the phone, taught me to make.

Ambivalence wasn't indifference. Ambivalence was irreverence.

I watched the flames, the soup simmering, and skimmed the self that resisted being

Renounced. Scrim of decoration. Scum of denial. To expect nothing was still to have

Expectations: a bowl I emptied and cleaned and refilled and emptied again.

My life was this now. I had to get used to it. To use it. I got rid of my past

Investment in the categories of *good* and *bad*. Survival was survival

In the end. In a drawer were various Tupperware and various lids.

Cause never matched consequence. This never belonged to that.

And yet I found sustenance and forms to contain it. I found the word

Effect meant the verb *cause* and the noun *consequence*. Everything wasn't and was.

Effect of running into someone with your musk of Old Spice and smoke
Meant I dissociated from myself. Memory was a matador. A bull charging through
I don't like modern psych language in poetry into a metaphor. The bodega on fire. I made a list of action items. Inhale. Exhale.
Verb followed by another verb. Someone triggering the automatic doors was enough

Cause for me to be in that room again. To feel your tongue turn in my mouth

And hear the ice cream truck. The song. I made a list of red objects.
The shelf of Hot Cheetos. The tray of red lighters. The fridge of Red Bull.
Noun followed by another noun. Inhale. Exhale. I repeated to myself that

Consequence was a sequence of contradictions. Contrivances. Controlling
Everything injured me more than the injury of what memory won't let me forget.

Wasn't the word for *injury* the same in Vietnamese as the word for *love*?

And stepping forward for a pack of Newports and some Tylenol, I thought if love
Was this remembering, this membrane between reliving and relieving, then what? So what.

it's not, right?

Was I wrong to believe that I could be loved after all

This time convinced I was the twisted pine, convinced I had to keep on
Remembering the desert wind, the flames that broke into and broke open

This body, that released from me another me, another

Membrane containing Pleasure and Death, planted beneath the ash
Between me and the human shore that, one day, will rescue me from this

Reliving, this pattern, season after season, of Death

And Pleasure, and suppose I lived to see myself alive, anew, finally
Relieving myself of my wish for the if in the middle of life, was I wrong

Then to believe that I could love someone else? Tell me

What love is to a survivor. Tell me love, like voice, can be wrung from violence
So that this—pine, wind, flame, seed, ash—might mean something, though

What that is, even if it's nothing in the end, I couldn't say.

What I withhold from my mother when she asks me what happened
That night before my twenty-first birthday I withhold to protect her.
    (Is this the explanation I offer myself?) As we continue along the Embarcadero,
Even as waves retreat from the seawall, as my mother takes my hand in hers
    —If not tenderly, then with her kind of tenderness—I assure myself
It's easier, with the truth, with those I love, to be spare than to be unsparing.
    Nothing hurts—not the waves racing in, not my mother releasing my hand

In the last light of the year, recounting as though an apology to me
    The story of what happened to her, how she assumed it would never
End—like asking forgiveness not for what had been done but for what hadn't.
    I guess this, too, is love. Indirection. Suppression. Silence. Pressing on.
Couldn't omission be admission? Couldn't an embankment be an embrace?

        ★

    (Say, roughly, now, the truth.) A man seeded me without consent. I bloomed.

Say cheese, the camera commands the octopus receding into the reef.

Roughly, then not so roughly, the octopus extends a tentacle.

Now the camera advances. Ruthless is the mind determined to capture

The truth about the mind, whatever that might be.

Truth reveals more about the viewer than the subject being viewed.

A man I loved said that my evolution was *unbelievable*. I kissed him and said that

Man and his failure to believe was exactly why I had to evolve.

[Seeded? Yes. Like a plot. Ceded? Absolutely not.] Like the octopus

Me confronting what could kill me was me confronting my life

Without reservation. The octopus lunges forward. *I do not*

Consent to this. Beak. Teeth. Venom. Grip. Reaching for the unknown

I unleashed my tentacle. I unleashed all my tentacles at once.

Bloomed. Blurred. *Let this photograph show that human nature is nature's cruelest invention.*

Bloomed after decades dormant. After dryness and heat. After the rainfall
Blurred the atmosphere. The desert a sea of gold and pink and purple.
Let sprout. Let butterflies and bees and hummingbirds. Let grow

This Desert Gold. This Gravel Ghost. This Golden Evening Primrose. This
Photograph of Notch-Leaf Phacelia rising three feet high from a bed of stone.
Show the way. Show salt flats and sand dunes and rock. Show faith

That a moment can be a monument. That the monumental can be this momentary.

Human was I who came back and still took for granted the abundance
Nature made known to me. Prince's Plume. Magnificent Lupine. My suffering
Is that I try to make my suffering beautiful, and I'm no beauty. I'm told that

Nature's an allegory in which the ego hides. Like the Dark-Throat Shooting Star
Cruelest was I who crossed Death Valley to the Valley of Life. By my own
Invention, I found a way. I'm no artifact. Between art and fact: I.

Invention slid into my mind tonight, like a formal feeling, just as
I slid my body into my bodysuit. It was August again.

Found in my purse was a boarding pass. And there I was looking through
A telescope in the fog-covered field as someone drew closer.

Way in the distance, the stars appeared. Still fixed. Still luminous.

I'm going to be far from my pain one day. I'm going to
No longer feel that pain but something new and just as merciless.

Artifact of the past. Artifice of the future. There I was in the tall grass
Between the choices I'd made and the choices I was given. The fog's ambivalent

Art made it so that I saw only what was in front of me.

And no matter what drew closer—the stranger in the field or the field itself,
Fact or fiction, my need or my desire—I had to focus on what I could see.

I see not stars but their light reaching across the distance between us.

THE CAVE

*pick up where we
left off from
within cave*

Done with darkness,
someone had the idea to fashion a lamp
from stone. Animal fat. Flint.

They held the lamp
in front of them. Light no longer
behind them. Light in front of them. Light flickering.

*Woah they beat
the allegory*

Retreating shadows revealed
curtains of stalactites. Calcite-rich clay.
Eroded moonmilk.

Someone had not so much arrived
at their destination
but for the time being decided

that where they were—where the idea had
taken them, where they permitted
the idea to take them, where they permitted themselves
to be taken—was just as good as anywhere

to be. (Sometimes that's all
there is: this.)

if you're gonna live...

Then someone had another idea.

They ground hematite in an ochre-stained shell.
They sucked the pigment into their mouth with a bird bone.
They swished the powder back and forth.
They became light-

headed. Between darkness and light
someone found a wall
history had set aside for them.

*You might as
well get high
and make art*

They placed their hand on the wall.
They blew paint on their hand.

Someone thought, *This was the best idea I've had.*

*I still think the urge
to wrap everything up in a clear
bow hurts the impact of the poetry*

58

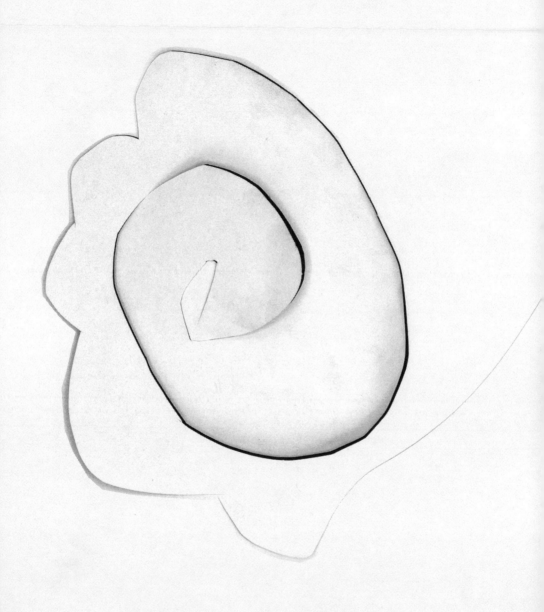

ENLIGHTENMENT

You illuminated me.

We see what we believe.
We believe what we see.

I close my eyes to open them.

Here's a lamp.
Here's oil for the lamp.

From me to you.

its about giving not receiving?

PROGRESS REPORT

rewriting personal history

I had a new form

The new form said *Name of survivor*.

The new form renamed me.

The new form was a form of renaming.

Renaming gave me new form.

The new form said *Relevant history*.

History could be relevant.

History could be irrelevant.

History had a form.

History was a form of renaming.

The new form said *Daily function*.

Days could be measured by and a measurement of history.

Function could be defined by and a definition of history.

Both had a form.

Both were a form of renaming.

The new form said *Identify triggers*.

Click of the key turning in the lock of the door.

The new form said *Identify recurring memories*.

Repetition of one foot placed in front of the other.

The new form said *Identify survival strategies*.

Pulling the string I thought was for the light.

I marked *Rationalizing*.

Ceiling fan whirring like helicopter blades.

I marked *Denial.*

Odor of Heineken and pubic sweat.

I marked *Fantasizing about the future.*

Altar where my mother and I knelt before Ngài Quán Thế Âm.

I marked *Obsessing about the past.*

Fresh oranges arranged in a glass bowl.

I marked *Compartmentalizing.*

Hallway from the living room to the bedroom.

I marked *Dissociating.*

My bed stripped of sheets.

I marked *Not eating.*

Stack of high school yearbooks.

I marked *Compulsive eating.*

Gym uniform embroidered with my name.

I marked *Not sleeping.*

Clang of the Science Fair trophy hitting the floor.

I marked *Compulsive sleeping.*

Poem I wrote in fifth grade rhyming the word *heart* with the word *start.*

I marked *Avoiding sex.*

Photograph of me sitting next to my father.

I marked *Compulsive sex.*

Photograph of the '93 Mazda MPV he reportedly turned into an ice cream truck.

I marked *Humor.*

Holes where the nails had been in the wall.

I marked *Self-harm.*

Wind through the window.

I marked *Caregiving.*

Alarm clock unplugged.

I marked *Drug use.*

The room emptied even of time.

I marked *Staying busy.*

The air as if on fire.

I marked *Controlling others.*

Pile of things to keep and pile of things to throw away.

I marked *Perfectionism.*

(Let go.)

I marked *Repeating abuse.*

The decision to keep nothing.

I marked *Suppression.*

(Set free.)

I marked *Creating chaos.*

Broom sweeping into the dustpan the need to hold on.

The new form said *Ways this strategy is useful to me.*

I chose a new start.

The new form said *Ways this strategy is damaging to me.*

I chose a new heart.

The new form said *Some things I want to change are.*

I left the field blank.

(Change me.)

I left the field.

(Change me.)

I left the blankness.

(Change me.)

The blank field was my answer.

new progression

trauma→symptom→healing

SCIENTIFIC METHOD

I think, if I could, I'd be anything else
in this world. *Mimosa pudica*. My leaves closing

when touched. I'd go back to 1729,
take for shelter the awful crypt Master kept me in

with only enough water to last between his visits,
during which he spoke not to but about me,

as though I lacked a mind, an appeal
for fellowship or feeling. I'd go back to him, a shadow

slithering in the dark. His eyes burning
like two moons monitoring a realm

where nothing exists, where everything was destroyed.
Both a problem of imagination. Obsessed

with the nature of things, Master observed that
even without knowledge of sunlight, true day
and true night, I sensed my proper sovereign
in heaven and served the source of my life

by rising and bowing with heliotropic devotion,
unfolding and folding according to its will.

I'm sure he hated me for that—bridled
consciousness, circadian rhythm—for I hated that too.

Yet I made him famous. His name written down in
history. Beware of me. I who survived

his experimentation. I who felt the fire of stars
despite this lonely toil, locked away as he played

god at his wet bench, seeker sullied by all
he seeks, his ego subordinating me, denying me

the ambivalence passing as affection
lavished upon his other houseplants: a seat on the sill

to bathe in shafts of gnat-swarmed August, happily
startled by my unremarkable nudity, my face

in the window. I'd go back to punish him
with clarity. What Master did to me

he did to himself because it was done to him
and to that which did it. We suffer _cycle of trauma_

as our sovereign suffers, forsaken as far as the eye
can see, the cost of seeing and being seen.

GALILEO

I thought I could stop
time by taking apart
the clock. Minute hand. Hour hand.

Nothing can keep. Nothing
is kept. Only kept track of. I felt

passing seconds
accumulate like dead calves
in a thunderstorm

of the mind no longer a mind
but a page torn
from the dictionary with the definition of *self*

effaced. I couldn't face it: the world moving

on as if nothing happened.
Everyone I knew got up. Got dressed.
Went to work. Went home.

There were parties. Ecstasy.
Hennessy. Dancing
around each other. Bluntness. Blunts

rolled to keep
thought after thought
from roiling

like wind across water—
coercing shapelessness into shape.

I put on my best face.
I was glamour. I was grammar.

Yet my best couldn't best my beast.

I, too, had been taken apart.
I didn't want to be
fixed. I wanted everything dismantled and useless

like me. Case. Wheel. Hands. Dial. Face.

THE SANTA ANA

Desert-born. Wild as corn.
    Head bitch.
        Itchy clit.
I throw a fit, and meteorologists report
    rising mercury.
        My Mercury
always in retrograde.
    I'm neither mercurial
        nor retro-chic.
I'm miraculous.
    Chickenshit.
        Cashing my checks.
Checking my balance.
    Overdraft. Override.
        OMG.
I die every time
    I'm touched.
        Everything I touch
erupts with flame.
    Everything got
        the hots for me.
I'm flamboyant.
    I'm a witch
        still burning.
I stake my life
    on my red dress.
        Redressed.
Retweeted. Right off
    the runway. So damn *Vogue*
        I make you dip.
Death-drop. So gorgeous
    I make you drop dead. Jesus.
        My winter will outlast
Anna Wintour.
    The only season
        is me. My sister.

Her steady hand.
        Her eye on the sparrows:
                my eyebrows.
Plumes she plucks
        with care I can't remember
                anybody giving me.
Her face so close
        to mine. She sees
                not what I am.
She sees what I can be.
        Symmetry. Asymmetry.
                I know I'm ugly.
I have no alibi.
        But to my chosen
                family—family
who chose me—
        I'm the most
                beautiful bitch
in the world. Behold
        my bitch face.
                My bitch glare.
My bitch hair.
        My bitch nails.
                My bitch toenails.
My new bitch brows.
        Pop quiz: Who's that bitch?
                That bitch,
bitch. That's me
        looking at myself
                for the first time!
My sister taking
        a step back. A step forward.
                This angle. That angle.
This is devotion.
        Attention. Revision.
                Precision.
A sister assisting her sister
        in becoming. Coming
                back from the dead.

Apocalypse. Apocrypha.
          We're the only testament.
                    We're the wind
the angels failed to stop
          from winding through Eden.
                    (*Bitch, you hungry.*)
Sodom.
          (*Bitch, look back.*)
                    Southern California.
(*Bitch, take this butter
          knife to your husband's neck.*)
                    Haven't you heard
us howling down the cliffs,
          swishing our hips
                    into the Cajón
like a lovesick coyote?
          All thrash. All ass.
                    Deep-throat. Whip-
lash. We bat our eyes,
          and Los Angeles lights up
                    like a cigarette.
Her American Spirit.   ⌉ bad choices
          My Newport.   ⌋
                    Ashtray to ashtray.
The greatest thing,
          my sister tells me, is being
                    our greatest thing.
Our greatest wish. My wish:
          I want to say
                    what happened to me.
I want a say
          in what happens to me.
                    Am I selfish
for wanting things
          to make sense? To matter?
                    To amount,
in the end, to something
          more than a tally

                    of days and nights?
If this bitch and her bitches
              must alone order and reorder
                    Heaven
—cutting a new cheek,
              contouring a new nose,
                    lining a new lip—
because even the almighty
              can be too self-
                    righteous to right
their mistakes, ignorant
              of ignorance,
                    then we demand
the highest seats
              in Heaven. Game over.
                    LOL. *(Sorry
not sorry!)* So wow. Very
              Mary. Go round up
                    your little lambs.
Nothing is safe
              from me. Try me.
                    Give me the trial
of the century.
              Give me Liberty.
                    Give me Death
Valley. I want
              all the flowers
                    kneeling.

This poem references the internet
too much! But its good I guess

JUDITH SLAYING HOLOFERNES: OIL ON CANVAS: ARTEMISIA GENTILESCHI: 1620

art history 101

I know better than to leave the house
    without my good dress. My good knife

like a crucifix between my stone breasts.
    Mother would have me whipped,

would have me kneeling on rice until I shrilled
    so loud I rang the church bells.

Didn't I tell you that elegance is our revenge?
    That there are neither victims nor victors

but the bitch we envy in the end? I am that bitch.
    I am dogged. I am so damned

not even Death wanted me. He sent me back
    after you'd sacked my body

the way your armies sacked my village, stacked
    our headless idols in the river ⬅ *Jews don't have idols??*

where our children impaled themselves
    on rocks. I exit night. I enter your tent

gilded in a bolt of stubborn sunlight. My sleeves
    already rolled up. I know they'll say

I'm a slut for showing this much skin.
    This irreverence for what is seen

when I ask to be seen. Look at me. My thighs
    lift from your thighs. My mouth

spits poison into your mouth. You nasty beauty.
    I am no beast. Still my blade

sliding clean through your thick neck
    while my maid keeps your blood off

me and my good dress will be a song
  the parish sings for centuries. Tell Mary.

Tell Eve. Tell Salome and David about me.
  Watch their faces, like yours, turn green.

Is this a reference to Ultralight Beam?

SCHEHERAZADE/SCHEHERAZADE

8

Far from the beginning. Nowhere
near the end. I'd lost count
of the nights I spent in that room, knowing no more

or less than I did thousands of nights ago, when I thought
knowledge still meant something
in what was then my relentless pursuit

of meaning, though I knew meaning
couldn't be found or given but made
from what typically, in my limited and limiting

poets love this concept

experience, presents as meaningless, just as the image
of the face in the mirror might've been
had I not likened the image to a swan in a lake

or said I was the lake. I was the swan.
The mirror. The face. What more was there to know?

9 *volta?*

After what had been a long journey
in silence, the driver asked me
    what I was doing there. I told him
I was a poet. I was there for a reading.
    I was going to read a poem I wrote
about Scheherazade. He asked me *write*
    to explain what I meant. I told him
the story—how my mother told it to me

    when I was a child, how I had no idea
it was her gift to me, how to survive
    we told the story of our survival.
He looked at me. I saw him look at me.
    Yours isn't just a story about survival.
He said, *Yours is a story about love.*

10

In my version of the story Scheherazade had no plan. As she waited for the king to come the moon rose. The candles burned. The moths gathered. In my version of the story

Scheherazade slipped from the bed. She, at the window, leaned into the wind like the tulips in the garden. There was loss at the heart of each blossom. In my version of the story

Scheherazade, bored with sex, with waiting, hour after hour, for her little death, asked if the king had heard about the child born to a woman named War. In my version of the story

Scheherazade said a man named Beauty abducted the child. Beauty left the child to die alone in a land where they couldn't speak or find a way home. In my version of the story

Scheherazade, pushing his hair from his face, informed the king that War brought fire down on every hill and valley, canyon and cliff, searching for the child. In my version of the story

Scheherazade, when the king doubted that someone would destroy everything in their path for another, asked if he wasn't also doing that because of love. In my version of the story

Scheherazade extinguished the candles. The smoke looked like moths in the moonlight. The king asked what love is. *This*, she answered. He asked what happened next. *And then—*

Getting some Judith/Holofernes
type vibes from this one

11

—just like that, that moment
    when he went limp
inside me, the torment

    of his body and his mind coming to a stop
as if a scorpion seeing a mouse
    in the desert, the tail like a whip

drawn back, the poisonous
    barb coming down but not before
the prey opened its jaws

    to take the sting, to tear
through the predator, sending a cry
    hundreds of feet into the night, the air

suddenly alive, all that I felt and denied
    was over. Just like that—

12

Once more, at the temple, sweeping

the courtyard, the leaves

like shrapnel or ships crossing a darkening sea, a memory

my mother recounts and recants, insisting

that, when she was taken to shore

by soldiers who did what she won't say they did

to her, she was spared

because she had promised her life to serve

Ngài Quán Thế Âm,

I got down on my knees

in front of the bodhisattva, my broom cast aside

like the sword belonging to the brigand who wore a necklace

of nine hundred and ninety-nine human fingers, and I

wiped the earth from her feet with my own hands.

13

How could I see
that book splayed on that desk
     like a fetal pig—

its legs clamped, its heart inside
     the pericardial membrane
—and not see myself

anatomy imagery reference to hospitalization? (handwritten, right margin)

     opened on the exam table
with my eyes closed

     as if refusing to accept that
which, after all this time, couldn't be
     redeemed. Known. Forgiven.

I couldn't accept that
     suffering is suffering.

Not redemption. Not knowledge. Not forgiveness.

          ★

Unlike some animals, some spiders and birds
for whom darkness is a way to hide, to disappear
until they want to be found, to lure a lover
or a kill, which, under a certain light, can be the same
depending on the desire, there are those who don't want
to be found. For them, for the fangtooth and the Pacific
blackdragon, moving through the darkness
of the deep sea, absorbing the light
into their bodies, darkness isn't the opposite of light.
Darkness *is* light. I used to believe that
I wanted to be found. I rented a room in a basement
where, with the door ajar, with me on all fours,
a man pretending to be my king could do what he wanted.
Darkness. Light. I'm not sure what I believe anymore.

          ★

conflict/indecision for future as poem wraps up (handwritten)

Reap. Pear. Pare. Aper.
These are versions of the word

   I won't say. The word
~~without which~~ there's no *speaker*.

                      ★

My mother's name is Chiến.

My father's name is Mỹ.

Chiến comes from the Vietnamese word for *war*.

Mỹ comes from the Vietnamese word for *beauty*.

I'm a child of war.

I'm a child of beauty.

Beauty took me from War.

Beauty left me.

War found me.

I left what I come from.

I found other wars and other beauties.

I took me from them.

I took me from me.

I took me with me.

                      ★

   The rules of the game were simple.
Run. Freeze when touched. Unfreeze when touched
   again. I froze like *The Ecstasy of Saint Teresa*. The angel
piercing my heart with his spear while the others ran.
   None willing to put their hands on me.
Is it an exaggeration to say I stayed
   there, stuck like that, while the game continued?
It's not an exaggeration:

I haven't moved since. I'm still waiting
for someone to touch me. To unfreeze me. Free me
   from what I am. From what I was
made and forced to be. What I accepted being
   to get what I wanted. The spear—its tip on fire—
in my heart. The rules I agreed to when I asked to play.

     ★

Surrender means *to give up* and *to give up*.   *[handwritten: not sonnet!]*

I gave up.

I didn't give up.

     ★

There's a clearing I go to in my mind   *[handwritten: orchard?]*
when I miss my sisters. I find them
there, with my mother, in the shadows of a tree
like the banyan that grew in my grandmother's front yard.
Past the clearing is a cliff I've never approached.   *[handwritten: Never been to Vietnam?]*
I'm approaching it now. From wherever the cliff leads down to
a hawk flies up. My sister says it's my grandmother.
I thought divestment would make me a pure soul.
But there's no purity. As long as I long for that   *[handwritten: from?]*
desire blemishes me. I'm marked
by grief and by the idea that something must emerge from grief.
The difference was not unlike that difference
between the fear I felt going toward the cliff
and the fear I feel—having gone—seeing what's beyond.

     ★

Chiến comes, too, from the Vietnamese word for *victory*.

     ★

When asked about where the world was
in my poems, I was embarrassed
   to answer that, for so long, I was incapable of writing
poems where my speaker participated

actively in the world. My speaker announced themself in
rooms where there was nothing and nobody else.

    That's where they felt safe. That's where I felt safe.
It wasn't that I thought beauty was propaganda

    or that I forgot how beautiful the world was
—Smooth Jazz 98.1 on a summer afternoon, the percussion of rain
    on the Pacific Coast Highway, the Santa Anas
racing like waves through my hair, his fingers
    when he drew them from my mouth . . .
It was just too much. I didn't know what to do.

      ★

Take it the king
I return to

in dreams
said, and I did,

not because
I realize now

so long after
the fact

I wanted to die
but because

despite everything,
the world I knew

as the world,
I wanted to live

      ★

A mystery is a story.

A story is a mirror.

A mirror is a poem.

A poem is a pattern.

A pattern is repetition.

Repetition is emphasis.

The emphasis being the reason for repetition.

Repetition is also a break in a pattern.

Breaking a pattern is the reason for a poem. volta!

A poem is a mirror

I use to look

not at but into myself.

My story.

Mystery.

★

There's a gate in the park. I light a cigarette
on a bench surrounded by the ruins
   of what might've been a castle
reflected in a pool with a fountain in the center.
   It's raining. The rain falls into the pool
as if falling back into the sky.
   Fire in my lungs. Cloud of smoke.
I want a life that can't be corrected

   by my imagination. As for why
Scheherazade emerged from her castle of night?
   She taught the king to love her.
She was the pool. He was the rain. Love was the gate.
   Whether love leads us out or leads us in
I'm uncertain. I'm correcting my imagination.

★

   I, too, will be victorious
like my mother. Like Scheherazade, I'll survive

   in the end. I'll survive the end.
Even when I was helpless, I wasn't hopeless.

★

And on a night like tonight, watching lightning
reach for whatever it could reach for,
waiting for the sound its reaching made, I hated my loneliness
more than I hated sex. What did I suppose
my life, alive and not just surviving, would look like?
Waking after the storm. Washing my face. Drawing my eyebrows
the way my sister had taught me to
so that I could go to my job and prove that
I'm more than what's taken. I'm more than what I give.
The storm didn't end. The lightning continued
as I removed my eyebrows. Washed my face. Tossed and turned
in my sleep. I heard the reaching. I thought
I had no example. No equal. But I had so much.
And yet, whatever my life was, only I could save it.

14

Always, I'm told, there's more
to know. To feel. To do. Today, before dawn,
I'm listening to the water

as I wash and dry and stack each spoon
atop the other, amused
by the exactitude of their design.

How such things exist in this world
where unbelievable things occur and recur
without design or exactitude

is no longer, at least to me, a matter
of how but of belief. Years ago
I learned of the painters who painted over   → *pentance/repentance*

their paintings. [Historians call it *pentimento*.
I call it *being alive*. Listen. You will understand me]

COPERNICUS

Who doesn't know how
doubt lifts the hem of its nightgown

to reveal another inch of thigh
before the face of faith?

I once didn't. I once thought I was
my own geometry,
my own geocentric planet

spinning like a ballerina, alone
at the center of the universe, at the command of a god
opening my music box
with his dirty mouth. He said,

Let there be light—
And I thought I was the light.

I was a man's failed imagination.

Now I know what appears
as the motion of Heaven
is just the motion of Earth.

Not stars.
Not whatever I want.

ORCHARD OF UNKNOWING

you gotta know before you can unknow

Where I run naked but for my snakeskin coat
so fast through wind I become the wind.

Where the flowers—opened, closed—tell me
things have happened. Are happening. Are about to.

More than the sum of its parts

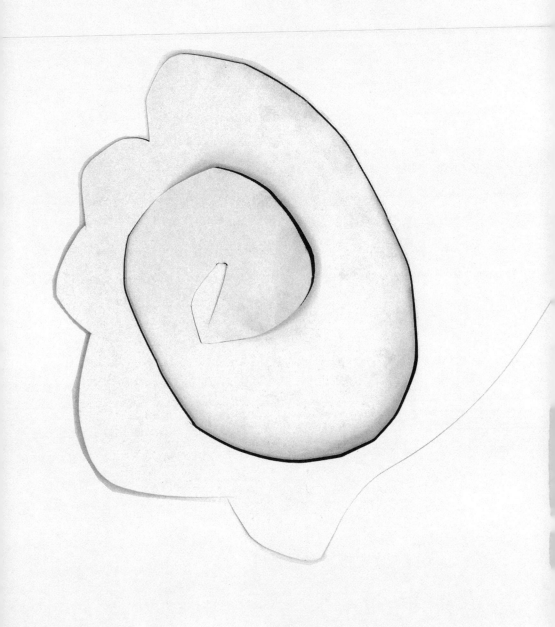

NOTES

"Orchard of Knowing" draws from an encounter between the Buddha and a brigand. In some traditions, the brigand is named Angulimala, which translates to "necklace of fingers," and is charged with collecting a thousand fingers by killing a thousand human beings so he can return from exile to his homeland. After collecting 999 fingers, the brigand is intercepted and converted by the Buddha.

★

"Incident Report" borrows its formal and rhetorical strategy from the poem "Study of Two Figures (Pasiphaë/Sado)," authored by Monica Youn in the February 2019 issue of *Poetry* magazine.

★

"Scheherazade/Scheherazade" draws from the Central and South Asian collection of stories known as *The Thousand and One Nights* or *The Arabian Nights*, wherein a king executes his wife and those she had been unfaithful to him with. He weds and executes a new wife each day until Scheherazade, the eldest daughter of the vizier, volunteers to marry him. During her evening with the king, Scheherazade begins telling a story. That next morning, arriving at the hour of her death, Scheherazade pauses the story on a cliff-hanger. The king delays her execution, eager for the story to continue, and does so for 1,001 nights. Some claim that the king falls in love with Scheherazade and spares her life. Others claim that the king doesn't simply fall in love but learns to love by listening to Scheherazade, and therefore Scheherazade saves herself.

Section 6 borrows the axiom "repetition is emphasis" from Mary Jo Bang.

★

"Scientific Method [Of the books he wrote about me . . .]" takes its persona from *De humani corporis fabrica libri septem* (*On the Fabric of the Human Body in Seven Books*), a set of human anatomy books authored by Andreas Vesalius at the University of Padua in 1543. The books used public dissection and woodcuts to represent human anatomy and repudiate previous anatomical studies. Several editions were reportedly bound in the skin of the cadavers that Vesalius had publicly dissected. The cadavers, obtained from execution sites and hospitals with the assistance of public and judicial authorities, often belonged to those who had occupied a marginalized status in life.

The term *Old Masters* is borrowed from the poem "Musée des Beaux Arts," authored by W. H. Auden in the collection *Another Time* (New York: Random House, 1940).

The line "They thought they knew . . ." adapts and augments the argument about knowledge from the poem "At the Fishhouses," authored by Elizabeth Bishop in the August 9, 1947, issue of *The New Yorker*.

★

"The Cave [Someone standing at the mouth . . .]" refers to Upper Paleolithic cave art dating back to approximately 35,000 years ago, as well as to the allegory of the cave from the dialogue *Republic*, authored by Plato in 375 BCE.

★

"Provenance" refers to the Santa Ana winds, also known as the devil winds, which contribute to regional wildfires throughout California.

★

"*Landscape with the Fall of Icarus*: Oil on Canvas: Pieter Bruegel the Elder: 1560" borrows the term *human position* also from the poem "Musée des Beaux Arts," authored by W. H. Auden.

★

"The First Law of Motion" refers to *Philosophiae naturalis principia mathematica* (*Mathematical Principles of Natural Philosophy*), a set of physical theories authored by Sir Isaac Newton in 1687. As announced by the title of each section, the first of the laws of motion argues that an object in motion stays in motion at the same speed and in the same direction until acted upon by an unbalanced force.

★

"Scientific Method [Of course I chose the terry cloth surrogate . . .]" takes its persona from a baby rhesus monkey experimented on by Harry Harlow at the University of Wisconsin–Madison in 1959. Testing the drive-reduction theory of attachment posed by Sigmund Freud, who asserted in 1939 that "love has its origin in attachment to the satisfied need for nourishment," Harlow separated eight baby rhesus monkeys from their mothers. He placed each in an individual cage with two surrogate mothers. The first was made of terry cloth. The second was made of wire. Although both provided the babies with milk, Harlow observed over 165 days that the baby rhesus monkeys preferred the terry cloth surrogate, holding on to it when an oddity, such as a mechanical teddy bear that marched and beat a drum, was introduced to the individual cages. This indicated that drive-reduction didn't drive attachment. Instead, Harlow believed that a sense of security, or an "internal working model," shaped the patterns of attachment.

★

"Year of the Monkey," in the section titled "Fall," adapts the line "At the center of my new life . . ." from the poem "The Wild Iris," authored by Louise Glück in the collection *The Wild Iris* (New York: Ecco, 1993), which says "from the center of my life came / a great fountain, deep blue / shadows on azure seawater."

The section titled "Winter" refers to Ngài Mục Kiền Liên. In some traditions, Ngài Mục Kiền Liên is named Maudgalyayana and is an original disciple of the Buddha. Following the death of his mother, Ngài Mục Kiền Liên asks the Buddha to help him locate the world into which she was reborn. The Buddha escorts him to the underworld. Ngài Mục Kiền Liên brings food for his mother. Because she refused to share with the other souls, the food bursts into flames in her mouth. The Buddha advises Ngài Mục Kiền Liên to repent on behalf of his mother, to transfer his karmic merits to her, so that she might be reborn into a better life.

The section titled "Spring" refers to a "morning in April 1975." This is April 30, 1975, also known as the Fall of Saigon, which marked the end of the Vietnam War and of the American War in Vietnam.

The lyrics "Thương anh thì thương rất nhiều . . ." are borrowed from the song "Gợi Giấc Mơ Xưa," popularized by Vũ Khanh.

★

"Lipstick Elegy" refers to the film *Raise the Red Lantern*, directed by Zhang Yimou and released in 1991. In the film, an educated woman, played by Gong Li, is forced to become the fourth wife, or third concubine, of a wealthy household when her father dies and leaves her family bankrupt.

The *Chú Đại Bi*, also known as the *Nilakantha Dharani* or the *Great Compassion Dharani*, is a Buddhist text associated with Ngài Quán Thế Âm. In some traditions, Ngài Quán Thế Âm is named Avalokitesvara, which translates to "the lord who gazes down," and is a bodhisattva resolved to remain in the human realm until all are emancipated from suffering. The *Chú Đại Bi* invokes the eighty-four incarnations of Ngài Quán Thế Âm. Some are gendered. Some are not.

★

"I See Not Stars but Their Light Reaching Across the Distance Between Us" is a nonce, or invented form. The form contains thirteen sections. Each section contains thirteen lines. The last line of each section contains thirteen words. The first word of the last line in section X becomes the first word of the first line in section Y. The second word of the last line in section X becomes the first word of the second line in section Y. This continues for the third through thirteenth words of the last line in section X and for the first words of the third through thirteenth lines in section Y.

This nonce form, which I call "the Hydra," modifies the imperatives that drive received forms like the sonnet, the sonnet crown, and the sestina to enact the interiority—the emotional and psychological life—of a survivor of trauma or extremity. Whereas a sonnet has fourteen lines, typically concluding on a conclusive couplet, the Hydra has only thirteen lines, to resist as much as possible the psychological impulse to reach for closure and certitude. Whereas a sonnet crown repeats, typically verbatim, the final line of sonnet X as the first line of sonnet Y, the Hydra repeats in order and verbatim the thirteen words in the final line of section X as the first words of the thirteen lines in section Y, to resist as much as possible the psychological impulse to import, cleanly and clearly, lessons learned from one experience to another. Instead, by dividing and deploying the thirteen words in the final line of section X as the respective first words of the thirteen lines in section Y, the Hydra submits that lessons learned from one experience are hardly ever cleanly and clearly imported to another, though they nevertheless remain present, informing—and haunting—each new experience. And whereas the sestina deploys word repetition at the end of the line, the Hydra deploys word repetition at the beginning of the line, to resist the psychological impulse to move from an unknown beginning to a known end. Instead, by moving from a known beginning to an unknown end, the Hydra enacts the experience of survivors embarking from the immediate aftermath of trauma or extremity toward an imagined future.

The rules of this nonce form, therefore, emerge from the belief that poetry isn't expression but enactment and also from the belief that every formal imperative must be driven by an emotional or psychological impulse.

"[Us in the car . . .]" refers to the album *Melodrama* by Lorde (Lava Records, 2017) and adapts the phrase "rush hour of being" from a statement made by Alfred Jarry, who said "living is the carnival of being."

"[Effect of running into someone with your musk . . .]" refers to the Vietnamese word for *injury* and the word for *love*, which can be translated as "vết thương" and "tình thương" respectively.

"[Was I wrong to believe . . .]" borrows the term *human shore* from the poem

"Nocturne," authored by Suji Kwock Kim in the collection *Notes from the Divided Country* (Baton Rouge: Louisiana State University Press, 2003).

"[*Say cheese*, the camera commands . . .]" refers to "bloomed," which is when the source or subject of illumination in a photograph saturates the pixels and causes smearing or streaking.

"[Bloomed after decades dormant . . .]" borrows the rhetorical strategy "Let . . ." from the poem "Let Birds," authored by Linda Gregg in the collection *Chosen by the Lion* (Saint Paul: Graywolf Press, 1994).

"[Invention slid into my mind tonight . . .]" borrows the term *formal feeling* from the poem "After great pain, a formal feeling comes," authored by Emily Dickinson in the collection *The Poems of Emily Dickinson*, edited by Ralph W. Franklin (Cambridge, MA: The Belknap Press of Harvard University Press, 1998).

★

"Enlightenment" draws from an encounter between the Buddha and a grandmother who, upon his arrival to her village, says that she has nothing in terms of food or money to offer but would offer the lamp that she has carried through the night to greet him. The Buddha tells her that the lamp—and the oil for the lamp—is more than enough.

★

"Progress Report" also borrows its formal and rhetorical strategy from the poem "Study of Two Figures (Pasiphaë/Sado)," authored by Monica Youn.

★

"Scientific Method [I think, if I could, I'd be anything else . . .]" takes its persona from the *Mimosa pudica*, also known as the touch-me-not or the shame plant, which was experimented on by Jean-Jacques d'Ortous de Mairan in 1729. After observing that the plant spread its leaves during the day and folded them at night, de Mairan isolated the plant in the complete darkness of his cupboard, where the plant continued to spread and fold its leaves without exposure to direct sunlight. De Mairan reportedly repeated this experiment through the summer months, perhaps to account for increasing and decreasing temperature, and helped establish a fundament of chronobiology: organisms such as the *Mimosa pudica* possess an internal circadian clock, or a circadian rhythm, that functions in anticipation of, rather than in reaction to, environmental changes.

★

The title "Galileo" refers to Galileo Galilei, who, in 1602, studied the properties of pendulums and found their function as timekeepers.

The phrase "coercing shapelessness into shape" is adapted from the phrase "to give to shapelessness a form" from the poem "Fray," authored by Carl Phillips in the collection *The Rest of Love* (New York: Farrar, Straus and Giroux, 2004).

★

"The Santa Ana" borrows the phrase "Give me Liberty . . ." from the speech delivered by Patrick Henry to the Second Virginia Convention at St. John's Church in Richmond, Virginia, in 1775.

★

"Scheherazade/Scheherazade," in section 13 "[How could I see . . .]," adapts the phrase "suffering is suffering" from the poem "90 North," authored by Randall Jarrell in the collection *The Completed Poems* (New York: Farrar, Straus and Giroux, 1981), wherein the speaker says, "Pain comes from the darkness / And we call it wisdom. It is pain."

"[The rules of the game . . .]" refers to *The Ecstasy of Saint Teresa*, which was designed and completed by Gian Lorenzo Bernini for the Cornaro Chapel of the Santa Maria della Vittoria in Rome, Italy, between 1647 and 1652.

"[There's a gate in the park . . .]" adapts "I want a life . . ." from the book *Anne of Green Gables*, authored by L. M. Montgomery (New York: Grosset and Dunlap, 1908). On page 26, traveling to Green Gables for the first time, Anne says, "It's the first thing I ever saw that couldn't be improved upon by imagination."

Section 14 adapts the phrase "Always, I'm told, there's more to know" from the poem "Illumination," authored by Natasha Trethewey in the collection *Thrall* (Boston: Houghton Mifflin Harcourt, 2012), and it refers to *pentimento* from the poem "Repentance," authored by Natasha Trethewey in the collection *Monument* (Boston: Houghton Mifflin Harcourt, 2018).

★

"Copernicus" refers to Nicolaus Copernicus, who authored *De revolutionibus orbium coelestium* (*On the Revolutions of the Celestial Spheres*) in 1543, the same year Andreas Vesalius published *De humani corporis fabrica libri septem*. The work helped shift the commonplace understanding of "the heavens" from a geocentric model with the Earth at the center to a heliocentric model with the Sun at the center. Likewise, it helped spark what historians now call the Enlightenment or Scientific Revolution, which contributed to overseas imperialism, by establishing fundaments for acquiring knowledge through the scientific method.

I believe a knowledge of resistance and liberation can be acquired, in poetry, through *the lyric method*.

ACKNOWLEDGMENTS

There is no sorcery without sacrifice—without support, solidarity in struggle, and the sustenance required to survive.

For believing in me, and for helping me enter my voice into literature and the historical record, I thank the editors of the following publications and institutions in which these poems, in earlier versions, first appeared: 92nd Street Y Unterberg Poetry Center, Academy of American Poets, *The Adroit Journal*, *The Boiler*, *Boston Review*, *Los Angeles Review of Books*, *Lit Hub*, *The Margins*, *The Nation*, *New England Review*, *The New Yorker*, *Ploughshares*, *Poetry*, *The Shade Journal*, and Split This Rock.

This book exists because of the teachers who taught me to read, to write, and most importantly, to think. I especially credit Mary Jo Bang, francine j. harris, and Carl Phillips for helping me become what Edwidge Danticat calls *an accident of literacy*. Thank you for teaching me that an actualized poem requires the actualization, or radical transformation, of the poet—that a poem is the discovery and enactment of an emotional and psychological investigation into the vexed interiority of a speaker, that *the interior is indeed political*—and that every poem, every time, in some miraculous way, must be an argument about the making of poetry itself.

I am grateful to the 92nd Street Y Unterberg Poetry Center, Asian American Writers' Workshop, Barnard Writing Collective and Barnumbia Slam, Bread Loaf Writers' Conference, Brooklyn Slam, Conversation Literary Festival, Diasporic Vietnamese Artist Network, Eliza So Fellowship (from Submittable, Plympton, and The Writer's Block), Fine Arts Work Center in Provincetown, The Home School, Kenyon Review Writers Workshop, Kundiman, Lambda Literary Foundation, Lightcap Farm Residency (from Writing By Writers), Lighthouse Writers Workshop, The Luminary and Andy Warhol Foundation for the Visual Arts, Massie & McQuilkin, Miami Writers Institute, Napa Valley Writers' Conference, National Endowment for the Arts, New Urban Arts, Nuyorican Poets Café, Pacific University MFA in Writing, Palm Beach Poetry Festival, Poets House, *Poetry* and the Poetry Foundation, Regional Arts Commission of St. Louis, The Soze Foundation, Split This Rock, Urban Arts Alliance and VerbQuake, Urban Word NYC, Vermont Studio Center, Voices of Our Nations Arts Foundation, Wallace Stegner Fellowship in Poetry at Stanford University, and both The Writing Program and Chancellor's Graduate Fellowship at Washington University in St. Louis for the sanctuary not only to reclaim but also to rebuild my life—to become, slowly, a better and more honest poet and person.

To Victory Matsui for daring me to dream bigger than I'd ever dreamt before.

To Rob McQuilkin for daring and dreaming, always, with me.

To Paul Slovak, Allie Merola, Kristina Fazzalaro, Patrick Nolan, and my incredible family at Penguin for this dream come true and for the many dreams, I hope, to come.

To Mary Jo Bang, Rick Barot, Rick Benjamin, Tina Chang, Jeremy Michael Clark, Colin Criss, Armen Davoudian, Joe Gutierrez, Victoria Hsu, Hieu Minh Nguyen, Nicole Sealey, Michael Shewmaker, and Callie Siskel for reading and editing earlier incarnations of this dream, this book, this garden of flowers.

To Alexander Chee, Dana Levin, Carl Phillips, Solmaz Sharif, and Natasha Trethewey for your flowers, in bloom, alongside mine.

To my aunties and siblings far and wide, and especially to my sisters, my Thousand Thousand Angels, for teaching me, again, how to love and for making this life, this Kingdom of *How Dare I*, worth living—and full of extraordinary surprises—season after season.

To the ancestors who came before, and who are here with me now, for watching over and conspiring with me in this and every life.

And to my mother, Trần Thi Chiến, for being the *original* Paula Tran, and for whom all the flowers, forever, kneel.

I love you.

Nam mô A di đà Phật.